Table of Contents

Rourke
Educational Media
rourkeeducationalmedia.com

Can you find these words?

brush

floss

gums

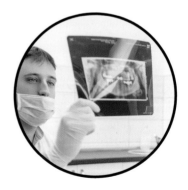

x-ray

Brush Your Teeth!

We have teeth.
Teeth help us chew.

Teeth help us talk.

We care for our teeth.

We **brush** our teeth.

We brush them every day.

Don't forget to **floss!**

floss

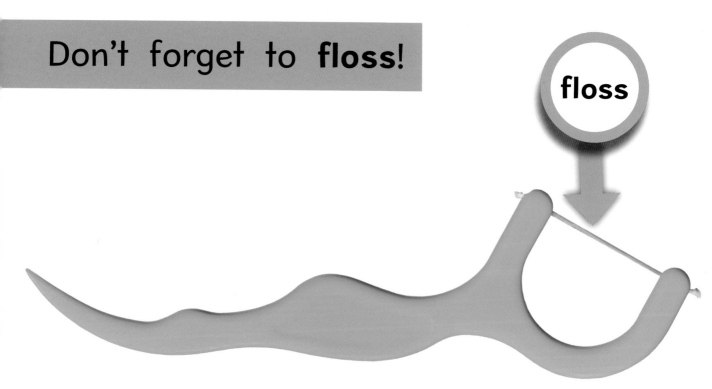

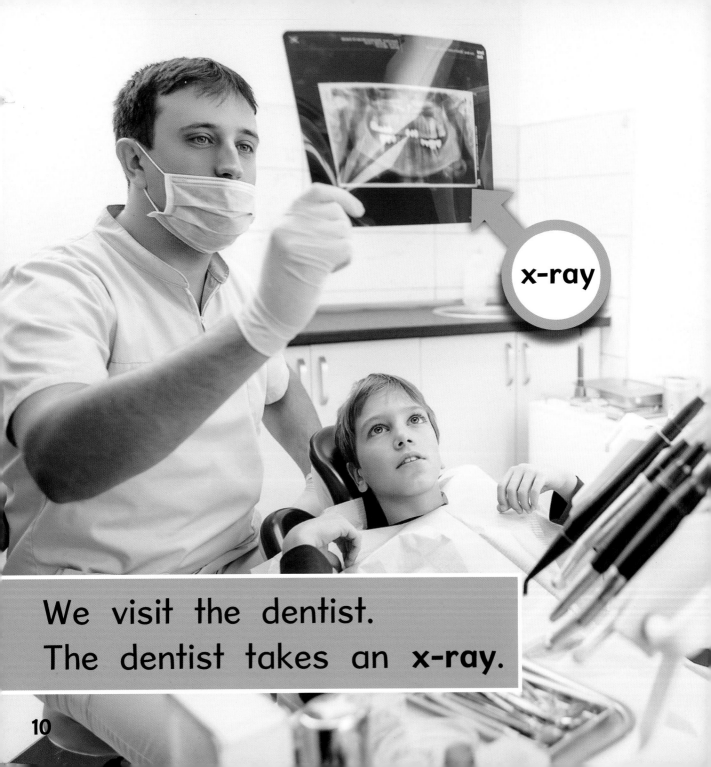

x-ray

We visit the dentist.
The dentist takes an **x-ray**.

The dentist cleans our teeth.

We eat healthy foods.

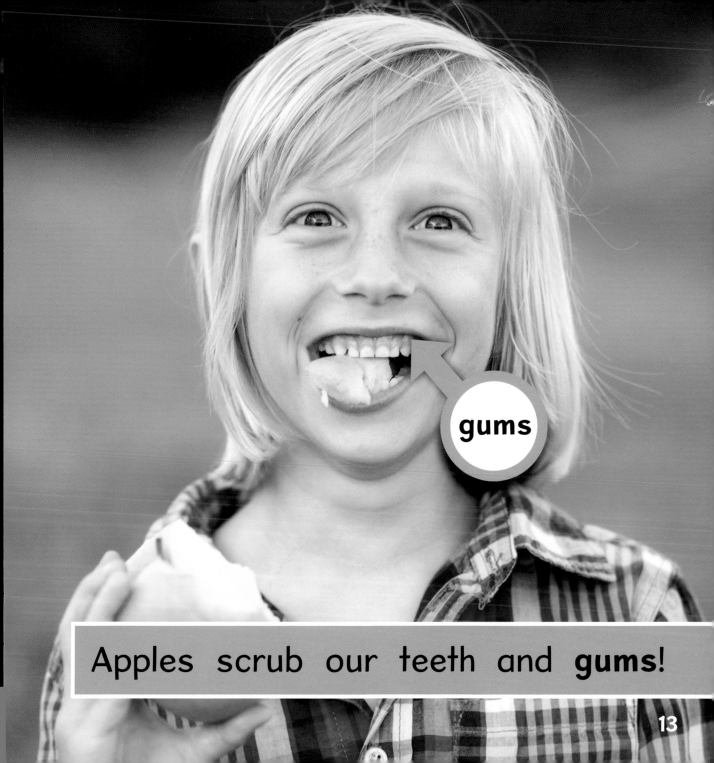

gums

Apples scrub our teeth and **gums**!

Did you find these words?

We **brush** our teeth.

Don't forget to **floss!**

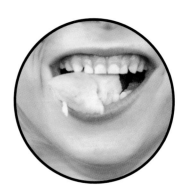

Apples scrub our teeth and **gums!**

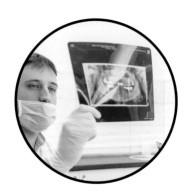

The dentist takes an **x-ray.**

Photo Glossary

 **brush** (bruhsh): To clean or groom something.

 **floss** (flahs): A thin strand of thread that cleans between your teeth.

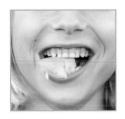 **gums** (guhms): The areas of firm, pink flesh around your teeth.

 **x-ray** (eks-ray): A picture of your teeth, bones, or organs inside your body.

Index

About the Author

Pete Jenkins loves to eat so he tries to take good care of his teeth. He never misses his dentist appointments and he even gets a goody bag if he has no cavities.

www.rourkeeducationalmedia.com

PHOTO CREDITS: Cover: ©Wavebreakmedia; p. 2,7,14,15: ©Jonathan Cohen; p. 2,8,14,15: ©You Touch Pix of EuToch; p. 2,13,14,15: ©tomazl; p. 2,10,14,15: ©hoozone; p. 3: ©Jason Doiy; p. 4: ©Jennifer_Sharp; p. 9: ©Pazargic Liviu; p. 11: ©LuckyBusiness; p. 12: ©Mark Bowden.

Edited by: Keli Sipperley
Cover design by: Kathy Walsh
Interior design by: Rhea Magaro-Wallace

Library of Congress PCN Data
Brush Your Teeth! / Pete Jenkins
(My World)
ISBN (hard cover)(alk. paper) 978-1-64156-202-7
ISBN (soft cover) 978-1-64156-258-4
ISBN (e-Book) 978-1-64156-307-9
Library of Congress Control Number: 2017957811

Printed in the United States of America, North Mankato, Minnesota